This Journal
belongs to

....

and

....

is going to help me fill it out every day

Kiki's I CAN Journal for Kids | Blue Edition

Published by: Babili Books, UK
Copyright ©2020 Francesca Hepton

All rights reserved. No part of this publication may be reproduced, stored in a retrieval system, or transmitted in any form or by any means, electronic, mechanical, photocopying, recording or otherwise without the prior permission of the author.

ISBN 978-1-8383005-0-0

A few words from Kiki

Make this journal your own. There are no rules. Don't worry about spelling. You can write and doodle where you like.

What you need to get started:
- Kiki's I CAN Journal
- Pens
- Pencils
- Colouring pens or pencils
- Stickers
- Glue stick
- Anything you want to stick in your journal

Anyone can keep a journal.

There is very little writing involved and only takes 5 to 7 minutes a day to complete. This is your space. A place of freedom.

Note to grown-ups*: This is not a diary. It is not a personal development tool. It is a proven way to illicit hidden feelings, promote emotional intelligence and consolidate a positive, confident attitude among children under 8. Its message and effects work indirectly. It is best presented as an activity book. Not something they have to do with the promise of changing or "fixing" them. No child is broken. Every child is beautiful. Let's help them see that.*

NURTURE A POSITIVE MINDSET THROUGH JOURNALING

Bringing a ray of sunshine into your life, every day.

Welcome to your I CAN Action Journal

This daily journal is designed as a playful introduction to both journaling and helping you develop a confident mindset.

Kiki and her friends will be with you every step of the way as you explore different activities that make you feel and be POSITIVE—like fun exercises, inspiring quotes, challenges and daily prompts.

Kiki inspires children to be confident.

When she puts on her red headband she can do anything!

What kind of a journal is this?

It is an action journal filled with daily activities designed to nurture self-belief and promote healthy habits.

Having a positive attitude to life is important if we want to be happy and confident. We tend to think about our problems a lot, worry about things that haven't happened yet, feel jealous, left out or that life is unfair. Journaling can change this. It keeps us on track of what we are doing and helps us stay more aware of our thoughts and actions.

By exercising your "positivity muscle" every day, you will soon find that not only do you feel happier, but so do the people around you. Life is much more enjoyable and easier with an "I can" attitude.

Bringing an I CAN attitude to situations helps us master seemingly difficult challenges. This gives us a sense of achievement, which boosts our self-esteem. In the end we become more confident about ourselves.

But the most important thing about this journal is that it is **yours**. Your very own magic toolkit for fun and feeling good about yourself every day. There are lots of activities waiting for you.

Come on, let's have some fun!

WHAT TO EXPECT IN THIS JOURNAL

This journal is divided into three months.
Every month follows the same format:

Week 1: Kiki's Challenge

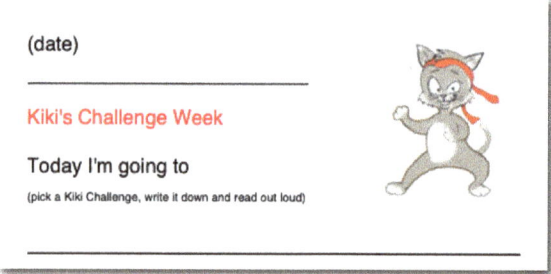

To inspire you to see things from a different perspective and become more aware.

Each challenge encourages you to step out of your normal zone and nurtures your confidence.

What I did differently, learned today:
1. I looked around me more
2. Felt calmer
3. Found a ladybird

Week 2: Dali's Doodles

A prompt to spark your creative flow.

A different question to strengthen your positivity or gratitude muscle.

Colouring in is a great way to find calm and be mindful

Your turn

Can't draw, won't draw?
Just colour in!

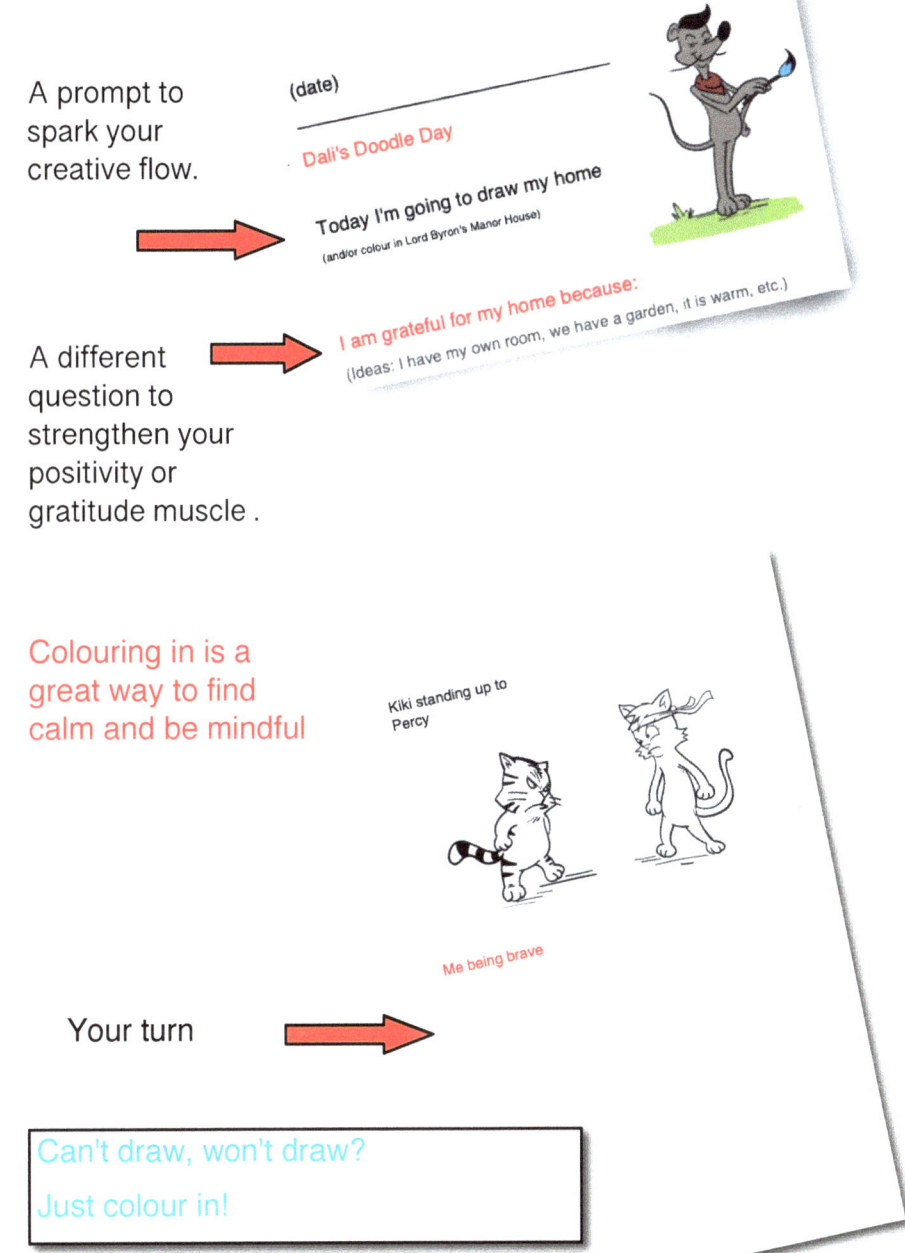

Week 3: "Mighty Me" Missions

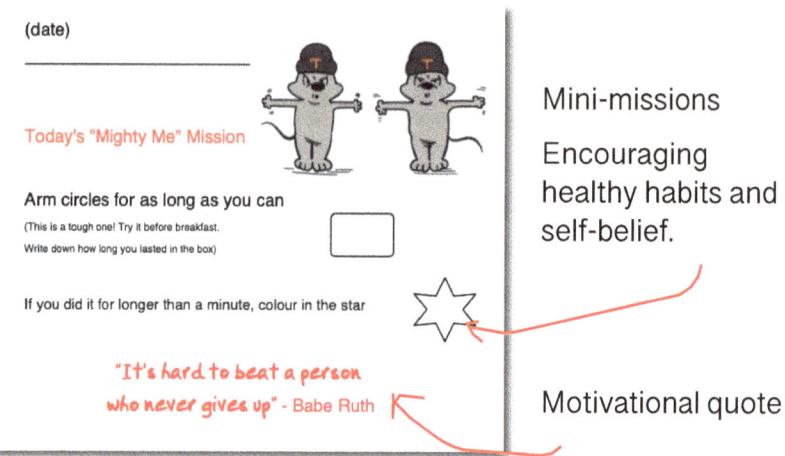

(date)
_____

Today's "Mighty Me" Mission

Arm circles for as long as you can

(This is a tough one! Try it before breakfast.
Write down how long you lasted in the box)

If you did it for longer than a minute, colour in the star

"It's hard to beat a person who never gives up" - Babe Ruth

Mini-missions

Encouraging healthy habits and self-belief.

Motivational quote

Exercising before breakfast has profound health benefits, boosts your mood and makes you more alert! No time? No worries. Exercise at any time is great for you!

These only take a few minutes and you can track your results. When you achieve a mission, it makes you feel more confident about yourself.

Bonus: Seeing how you improve month after month, spurs you on to do more and be even better every time!

MICRO-WINS LEAD TO BIG WINS

Week 4: Kiki's Caring Kids

Learning to care for yourself, others and the environment.

Month 1: Self-care

Month 2: Acts of Kindness

Month 3: Giving Back

Promotes self-love and love for others.

Complete 7 tasks...   ... to earn your certificate:

ACT OF SELF-CARE	STAMP / STICKER
Play outside for 20 minutes	
Sit quietly for 5 minutes	
No screen-time for 1 evening	
Try to meditate for 5 minutes	
Get 8 hours sleep	
Try yoga (for 10 minutes)	
Have a bath - with bubbles!	
Try a new vegetable	
Try a new fruit	
Read / listen to a story for 20 mins	

ACT OF SELF-CARE	STAMP / STICKER
Write down 3 things you are good at	
Drink 4 glasses of water - not all at once :)	
Write down 3 things that make you special	
Exercise for 20 minutes (games or cardio)	
Write down 3 things you like about yourself	
No crisps, fizzy drinks, chocolate or sweets	
Dress up smart for dinner and style your hair	

MEET KIKI AND HER FRIENDS

from Sleepy Meadow

(...the grumpy and evil-looking ones are the Farmies who live on Murk Farm!)

* Kiki and Friends adventure stories for early readers are available from all major bookstores and amazon. Visit their website for more information: www.kikiandfriends.co.uk

You don't have to read the stories to do this journal.

LET'S GET STARTED AND HAVE SOME FUN!!

Kiki and Friends* are waiting inside to help you every step of the way!

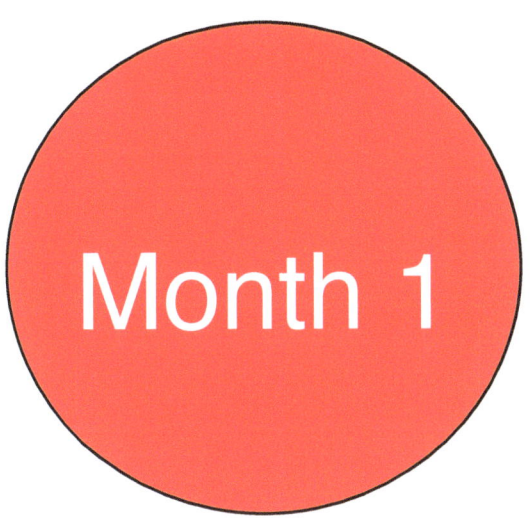

Month 1

Come on turn the page, let's get going! I'm ready!

Kiki is in charge of this week and she has some challenges for you!

Step 1

Cut out the words on the page opposite.

Step 2

Fold up the bits of paper and put them in a box or jar labelled:

"Kiki's Challenge Box"

(You can use an empty tissue box)

Step 3

Pick one piece of paper out every morning for a week and write it down in your journal.

Step 4

Read it out loud and complete the mission all day:

Example: Today I am going to be caring

Step 5

In the evening write down what was different about your day and/or what you learned.

Keep the box or jar in a safe place for next month.
(You can even add your own missions! Or visit www.kikiandfriends.co.uk to download more under FREE STUFF)

KIKI'S DAILY INTENTION CARDS

dream big	LOOK FOR FUNNY THINGS	be myself
just go for it	ask why	DO MY BEST
BE KIND	be thankful	create
ACT LIKE A WINNER	trust myself	follow my heart
be stronger	TRY HARDER	be clear
be honest	LOOK FOR RED THINGS	BE LIKE MY HERO
SMILE MORE	stop & listen	CONFIDENT

KIKI'S CHALLENGE

(date)

_____

Kiki's Challenge Week

In the morning: (pick a Kiki Challenge, write it down and read it out loud)

Today I'm going to

_____

Today I am looking forward to

_____

_____

_____

How am I feeling today? (colour in or draw your own)

HAPPY   SERIOUS   CREATIVE   SAD   HUNGRY

In the evening: think about your challenge

What did I do differently / learn / find today?

(date)

_____

Kiki's Challenge Week

Today I'm going to
(pick a Kiki Challenge, write it down and read out loud)

_____

Today I am looking forward to

_____

_____

_____

How do I feel? (colour in or draw your own)

CONFIDENT   HUNGRY   CLEVER   SERIOUS   EXCITED

What did I do differently / learn / find today?

I am the only ME!

(date)

_____

Kiki's Challenge Week

Today I'm going to

(pick a Kiki Challenge, write it down and read out loud)

_____

Today I am looking forward to

_____

_____

_____

How do I feel? (colour in or draw your own)

HAPPY   SERIOUS   CREATIVE   SAD   HUNGRY

What did I do differently / learn / find today?

(date)

_____

Kiki's Challenge Week

Today I'm going to

(pick a Kiki Challenge box, write it down and read out loud)

_____

Today I am looking forward to

_____

_____

_____

How do I feel? (colour in or draw your own)

CLEVER   CROSS   HUNGRY   EXCITED   WORRIED

What did I do differently / learn / find today?

(date)

_____

Kiki's Challenge Week

Today I'm going to

(pick a Kiki Challenge box, write it down and read out loud)

I never give up

_____

Today I am looking forward to

_____

_____

_____

How do I feel? (colour in or draw your own)

CONFIDENT   CROSS   CLEVER   HUNGRY   EXCITED

What did I do differently / learn / find today?

(date)

_____

Kiki's Challenge Week

Today I'm going to

(pick a Kiki Challenge, write it down and read out loud)

I bring joy to others

_____

Today I am looking forward to

_____

_____

_____

How do I feel? (colour in or draw your own)

CONFIDENT   CROSS   CLEVER   HUNGRY   EXCITED

What did I do differently / learn / find today?

(date)

_____

Kiki's Challenge Week

Today I'm going to

(pick a Kiki Challenge, write it down and read out loud)

_____

Today I am looking forward to

_____

_____

_____

How do I feel? (colour in or draw your own)

HAPPY   SAD   CREATIVE   WORRIED   CONFIDENT

What did I do differently / learn / find today?

(date)

_____

Dali's Doodle Day

Today I'm going to draw my home

(and/or colour in Lord Byron's Manor House)

I am grateful for my home because:

(Ideas: I have my own room, we have a garden, it is warm, etc.)

_____

_____

_____

_____

_____

How do I feel? (colour in or draw your own)

CONFIDENT   HUNGRY   CLEVER   SERIOUS   EXCITED

Manor House

(spooky house where Lord Byron lives!)

My home:

(date)

_____

Dali's Doodle Day

Today I'm going to draw me with a unicorn horn

(and/or colour in Banjo with a unicorn horn)

My favourite animal is:

_____

_____

Can you draw it?

How do I feel? (colour in or draw your own)

HAPPY   SAD   CREATIVE   WORRIED   CONFIDENT

Banjo with a unicorn
horn hairdo

Me with a unicorn hairdo:

(date)

_____

Dali's Doodle Day

Today I'm going to draw me drinking

(and/or colour in Piero drinking)

My 3 favourite drinks are:

_____

_____

_____

_____

_____

How do I feel? (colour in or draw your own)

CLEVER	CROSS	HUNGRY	EXCITED	WORRIED

Piero drinking with a straw

Me drinking with a straw:

(date)

_____

Dali's Doodle Day

Today I'm going to draw me helping a friend

(and/or colour in Kiki saving Poe)

Today I helped *(you can list more than one person!)*

_____

_____

_____

_____

_____

_____

How do I feel? *(colour in or draw your own)*

HAPPY   SAD   CREATIVE   WORRIED   HUNGRY

Kiki saving Poe

Me saving my friend:

(date)

_____

Dali's Doodle Day

Today I'm going to draw me in a silly place

(and/or colour in Allan in the washing machine)

3 things or people that make me laugh or smile:

_____

_____

_____

_____

_____

How do I feel? (colour in or draw your own)

CONFIDENT   CROSS   CLEVER   HUNGRY   EXCITED

Allan in the washing machine

Me in a silly place:

(date)

_____

Dali's Doodle Day

Today I'm going to draw me in a tree or outdoors

(and/or colour in Kiki up a tree)

I am good at:

(running, skipping, jumping climbing.... you can choose more than one!)

_____

_____

_____

_____

_____

How do I feel? (colour in or draw your own)

HAPPY   SERIOUS   CREATIVE   SAD   HUNGRY

Kiki up a tree keeping an eye on Banjo

Me outdoors:

(date)

_____

Dali's Doodle Day

Today I'm going to draw me listening to a friend

(and/or colour in Tiny and Titch listening to Piero)

Today I listened to (you can list more than one person!)

_____

_____

_____

_____

_____

How do I feel? (colour in or draw your own)

CONFIDENT   SERIOUS   CLEVER   SAD   EXCITED

Tiny and Titch listening to Piero

Me listening to a friend in need:

(date)

_____

Banjo's Surprise Smoothie

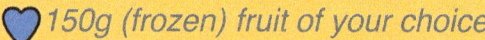

Banjo's Bonus!!

♥
    250 ml oat milk
♥ *150g (frozen) fruit of your choice*
    1 scoop plain yoghurt or vanilla ice cream
    3-4 ice cubes   (chocolate shavings optional)

Draw your surprise smoothie:

Colour in the star if you made and tried Banjo's Surprise Smoothie

(date)

_____

Today's "Mighty Me" Mission

Dance all out for 2 minutes

(Yay fun time! Try before breakfast.
Tick the box if you did this)

"You've gotta dance like there's nobody watching." - William W. Purkey

How do I feel? (colour in or draw your own)

SAD   HAPPY   CREATIVE   CONFIDENT

Fill in the blank space with your name:

Kiki thinks _____ is an awesome dancer. Keep it up you superstar!

(date)

_____

Today's "Mighty Me" Mission

Jumping Jacks for 1 minute

(Try to do this before breakfast.
Write down how many you did in the box)

If you did it for longer than a minute, colour in the star

"The secret to getting ahead is getting started." - Mark Twain

How do I feel? (colour in or draw your own)

CONFIDENT   HUNGRY   CLEVER   SERIOUS   EXCITED

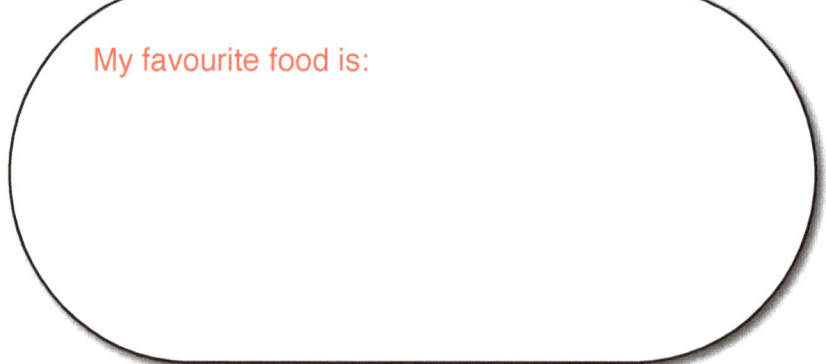

My favourite food is:

(date)

_____

Today's "Mighty Me" Mission

Arm circles for as long as you can

(This is a tough one! Try it before breakfast.
Write down how long you lasted in the box)

If you did it for longer than a minute, colour in the star

"It's hard to beat a person who never gives up" - Babe Ruth

How do I feel? (colour in or draw your own)

Somebody you could help or already do help:

(date)

_____

Today's "Mighty Me" Mission

Balance on your right leg

(Try to do this before breakfast.
Write down how long you did this for in the box)

If you did it for longer than a minute, colour in the star

"Everything you can imagine is real." - Pablo Picasso

How do I feel? (colour in or draw your own)

HAPPY   SAD   CREATIVE   WORRIED   CONFIDENT

Somebody who helps look after me:

(date)

_____

Today's "Mighty Me" Mission

Balance on your left leg

(Try to do this before breakfast.
Write down how long you did this for in the box)

If you did it for longer than a minute, colour in the star

"Believe strongly in yourself and go beyond limitations." - Arnold Schwarzenegger

How do I feel? (colour in or draw your own)

CONFIDENT   SERIOUS   CLEVER   SAD   EXCITED

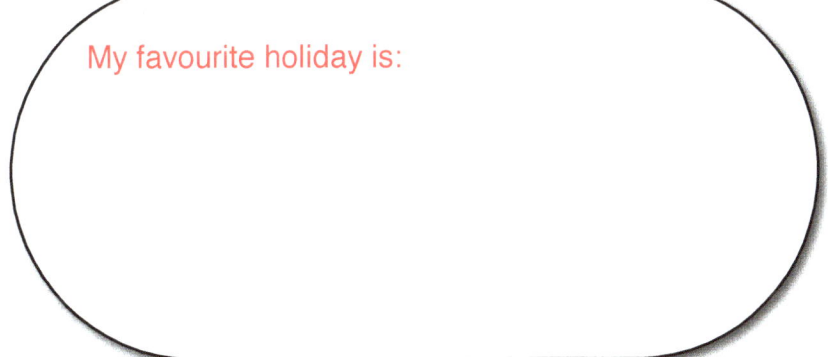

My favourite holiday is:

(date)

_____

Today's "Mighty Me" Mission

Balance on your right leg - with your eyes closed!

(Try to do this before breakfast.
Write down how long you did this for in the box)

If you did it for longer than a minute, colour in the star

"Whatever you are, be a good one." - Abraham Lincoln

How do I feel? (colour in or draw your own)

SAD   HAPPY   CREATIVE   CONFIDENT   _____

When it's raining I like to:

(date)

_____

Today's "Mighty Me" Mission

Balance on your left leg - with your eyes closed!

(Try to do this before breakfast.
Write down how long you did this for in the box)

If you did it for longer than a minute, colour in the star

"Impossible is just an opinion."
— Paulo Coelho

How do I feel? (colour in or draw your own)

CLEVER　　CROSS　　HUNGRY　　EXCITED　　WORRIED

The best thing about school:

Kiki's Caring Kids Challenge

ACTS OF SELF-CARE

Choose 7 acts of self-care from the table opposite. Over the next week you will do 1 every day. You will need to prove you have done them so your grown-up helper can sign them off with a stamp or sticker. (You can always do more if you like.)

Try as hard as you can, and you will earn your Certificate of Achievement at the end of the week* – plus you may notice how much happier and better you feel!!

*Cut out the certificate at the end of this week's section or visit www.kikiandfriends.co.uk to download a free A4 copy (under FREE STUFF) to print out.

ACTS OF SELF-CARE

ACT OF SELF-CARE	STAMP / STICKER	ACT OF SELF-CARE	STAMP / STICKER
Play outside for 20 minutes		Write down 3 things you are good at	
Sit quietly for 5 minutes			
No screen-time for 1 evening		Drink 4 glasses of water - not all at once :)	
Try to meditate for 5 minutes		Write down 3 things that make you special	
Get 8 hours sleep			
Try yoga (for 10 minutes)		Exercise for 20 minutes (games or cardio)	
Have a bath - with bubbles!		Write down 3 things you like about yourself	
Try a new vegetable		No crisps, fizzy drinks, chocolate or sweets	
Try a new fruit			
Read / listen to a story for 20 mins		Dress up smart for dinner and style your hair	

(date)

_____

My act of self-care today is:

(write or draw it)

Self-care means:

"Taking care of your physical body and mental health."

What am I looking forward to today?

_____

_____

_____

(date)

_____

My act of self-care today is:

(write or draw it)

Self-care means:

"Listening to what you need.

Noticing how you feel and respecting that."

Think of something good that happened today or yesterday:

_____

_____

_____

(date)

_____

My act of self-care today is:
(write or draw it)

Self-care means:

"Filling yourself with healthy fuel for your mind and body."

What am I looking forward to today?

_____

_____

_____

(date)

_____

My act of self-care today is:

(write or draw it)

Self-care means:

"Talking kindly to yourself and saying nice things to yourself."

Think of something good that happened today or yesterday:

_____

_____

_____

(date)

_____

My act of self-care today is:

(write or draw it)

Self-care means:

"Being kind to yourself and making time for you."

What am I looking forward to today?

_____

_____

_____

_____ (date)

My act of self-care today is:
(write or draw it)

Self-care means:

"Taking care of your emotions. Cry if you need to and laugh as much as possible."

Think of something good that happened today or yesterday:

_____

_____

_____

(date)

_____

My act of self-care today is:

(write or draw it)

Self-care means:

"Treating yourself like a friend."

Look in the mirror and say:

"I'm doing a great job."

What am I looking forward to today?

_____

_____

_____

Well done! You did 7 nice things for yourself. Don't you feel great?! Cut out your certificate or download an A4 poster from www.kikiandfriends.co.uk FREE STUFF

A HEALTHY START

KIKI & FRIENDS

INVITATION TO LOOK AFTER YOURSELF

Congratulations! You have demonstrated that you have the positive and caring attitude towards yourself to be a healthy person

Certificate of Achievement

This is to certify that

....

has completed a 7-day challenge in the
Kiki Self-Care program and is hereby awarded
the invitation to be the healthiest version of themselves

Parent/Carer

....

Signed

....

Date ....

Your name

....

Signed

....

Date ....

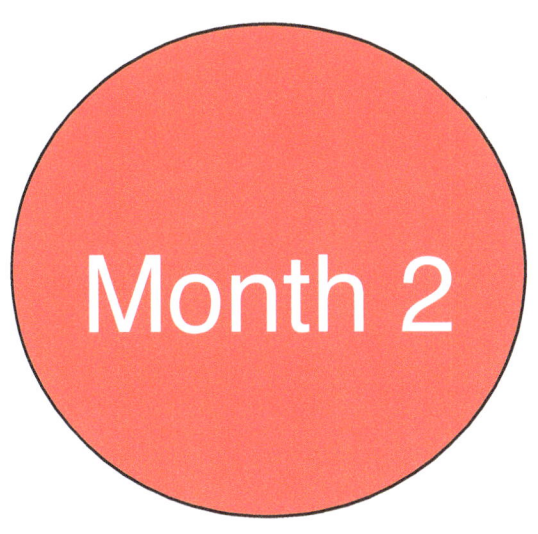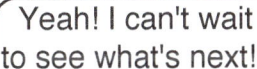

(date)

_____

Kiki's Challenge Week

Today I'm going to

(pick a Kiki Challenge, write it down and read out loud)

_____

How do I feel? (colour in or draw your own)

SERIOUS   CROSS   CLEVER   CONFIDENT

SAD   HAPPY   CREATIVE   _____

In the evening: think about your challenge

What did I do differently / learn / find today?

(date)

_____

Kiki's Challenge Week

Today I'm going to

(pick a Kiki Challenge, write it down and read out loud)

_____

What am I looking forward to today?

_____

_____

_____

How do I feel? (colour in or draw your own)

HAPPY   SERIOUS   CREATIVE   SAD   HUNGRY

What did I do differently / learn / find today?

(date)

_____

Kiki's Challenge Week

Today I'm going to

(pick a Kiki Challenge , write it down and read out loud)

_____

What am I looking forward to today?

_____

_____

_____

How do I feel? (colour in or draw your own)

CONFIDENT   SERIOUS   CLEVER   SAD   EXCITED

What did I do differently / learn / find today?

(date)

_____

Kiki's Challenge Week

Today I'm going to

(pick a Kiki Challenge , write it down and read out loud)

_____

What am I looking forward to today?

_____

_____

_____

How do I feel? (colour in or draw your own)

CLEVER   CROSS   HUNGRY   EXCITED   WORRIED

What did I do differently / learn / find today?

(date)

_____

Kiki's Challenge Week

Today I'm going to
(pick a Kiki Challenge, write it down and read out loud)

_____

What am I looking forward to today?

_____

_____

_____

How do I feel? (colour in or draw your own)

HAPPY — SAD — CREATIVE — WORRIED — CONFIDENT

What did I do differently / learn / find today?

(date)

_____

Kiki's Challenge Week

Today I'm going to

(pick a Kiki Challenge, write it down and read out loud)

_____

What am I looking forward to today?

_____

_____

_____

How do I feel? (colour in or draw your own)

It's a great day today!

CONFIDENT　　HUNGRY　　CLEVER　　SERIOUS　　EXCITED

What did I do differently / learn / find today?

(date)

_____

Kiki's Challenge Week

Today I'm going to

(pick a Kiki Challenge, write it down and read out loud)

_____

What am I looking forward to today?

_____

_____

_____

How do I feel? (colour in or draw your own)

CLEVER   CROSS   HUNGRY   EXCITED   WORRIED

What did I do differently / learn / find today?

(date)

_____

Dali's Doodle Day

Today I'm going to draw me looking smart

(and/or colour in Allan disguised as Piero)

3 things I like about my body:

(my hair, my fingers when I play an instrument, my legs when I run, my eyes, my smile, my belly button...)

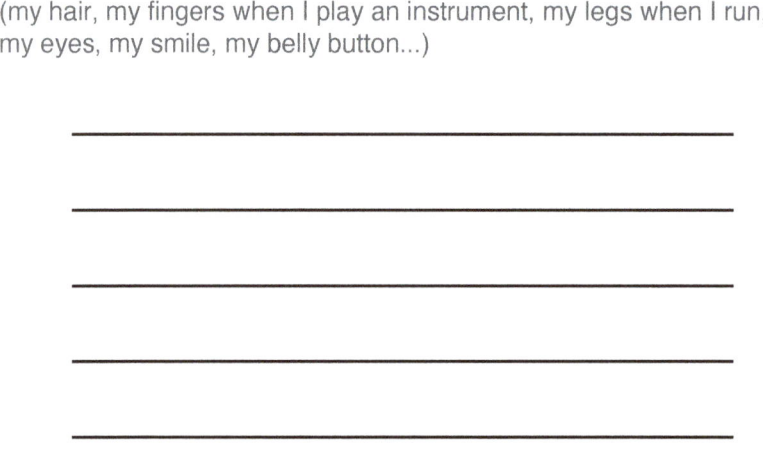

_____

_____

_____

_____

_____

_____

How do I feel? (colour in or draw your own)

CONFIDENT   HUNGRY   CLEVER   SERIOUS   EXCITED

Allan disguised as Piero

Me looking really smart:

(date)

_____

Dali's Doodle Day

Today I'm going to draw me relaxing

(and/or colour in Kiki relaxing by the window)

3 things I like doing, that make me feel good:

(reading, walking in the woods, watching a funny movie, singing, playing with my friends, listening to music...)

_____

_____

_____

_____

_____

How do I feel? (colour in or draw your own)

HAPPY   SAD   CREATIVE   WORRIED   CONFIDENT

Kiki relaxing by the window

Me relaxing:

(date)

_____

Dali's Doodle Day

Today I'm going to draw me spinning super-fast

(and/or colour in Kiki spinning like a tornado)

If I were Kiki, my superpower would be:

_____

_____

_____

_____

_____

How do I feel? (colour in or draw your own)

CLEVER   CROSS   HUNGRY   EXCITED   WORRIED

Kiki being amazing - spinning super fast

Me being amazing:

(date)

_____

Dali's Doodle Day

Today I'm going to draw me playing cards

(and/or colour in the Farmies playing cards)

My favourite games are:

(charades, Pictionary, board game, card game, bingo, Twister...)

_____

_____

_____

_____

_____

How do I feel? (colour in or draw your own)

HAPPY   SERIOUS   CREATIVE   SAD   HUNGRY

The Farmies playing cards

Me playing a game:

(date)

_____

Dali's Doodle Day

Today I'm going to draw me playing or watching TV

(and/or colour in Edgar, Allan and Poe playing)

My favourite computer game and/or TV show:

_____
_____
_____
_____
_____

How do I feel? (colour in or draw your own)

CONFIDENT   SERIOUS   CLEVER   SAD   EXCITED

Edgar, Allan and Poe playing

Me playing / watching TV:

(date)

_____

Dali's Doodle Day

Today I'm going to draw me and my (pretend) twin

(and/or colour in Tiny and Titch)

If I could be anyone, I would be:

_____

_____

How do I feel? (colour in or draw your own)

HAPPY   SAD   CREATIVE   WORRIED   HUNGRY

My favourite (super)hero is:

Twins: Tiny and Titch

Me and my (pretend) twin:

(date)

_____

Dali's Doodle Day

Today I'm going to draw my family

(and/or colour in Kiki and Friends family portrait)

I love my family because:

(they make me feel special, they hug me, they make me feel loved, they listen to me, we laugh together, we make stuff together...)

_____

_____

_____

_____

How do I feel? (colour in or draw your own)

CLEVER   CROSS   HUNGRY   EXCITED   WORRIED

My family:

(date)

_____

Today's "Mighty Me" Mission

Jumping Jacks for 1 minute

(Try to do this before breakfast.
Write down how many you did in the box)

If you beat your score from last month, colour in the star

"Don't let anyone dull your sparkle."

How do I feel? (colour in or draw your own)

CONFIDENT   CROSS   CLEVER   HUNGRY   EXCITED

The best thing about your bedroom:

(date)

_____

Today's "Mighty Me" Mission

Arm circles for as long as you can

(This is a tough one! Try it before breakfast.
Write down how long you lasted in the box)

If you beat your score from last month, colour in the star

"Nobody else is you and that is your superpower."

How do I feel? (colour in or draw your own)

What would you invent to make life better?

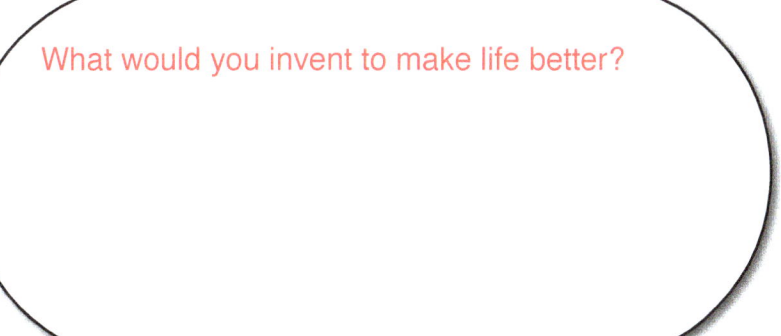

(date)

_____

Today's "Mighty Me" Mission

Balance on your right leg

(Try to do this before breakfast.
Write down how long you did this for in the box)

If you beat your score from last month, colour in the star

"Wake up. Be the best you can be. Repeat daily."

How do I feel? (colour in or draw your own)

CONFIDENT   SERIOUS   CLEVER   SAD   EXCITED

Someone who was kind to you today:

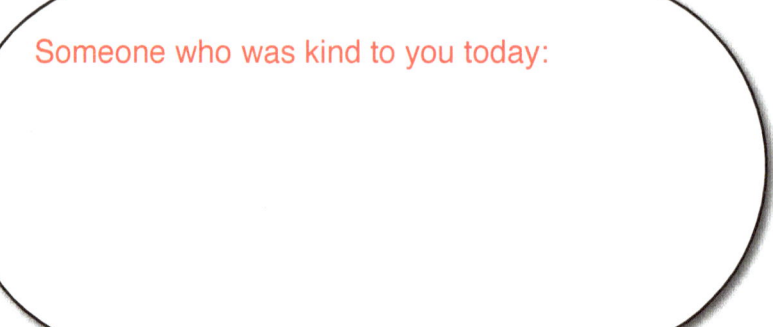

(date)

_____

Today's "Mighty Me" Mission

Balance on your left leg

(Try to do this before breakfast.
Write down how long you did this for in the box)

If you beat your score from last month, colour in the star

"Take care of your body. You're going to be in it your whole life."

How do I feel? (colour in or draw your own)

HAPPY   SERIOUS   CREATIVE   SAD   HUNGRY

Something that made you smile today:

(date)

_____

Today's "Mighty Me" Mission

Balance on your right leg - with your eyes closed!

(Try to do this before breakfast.
Write down how long you did this for in the box)

If you beat your score from last month, colour in the star

"Life is amazing. And so are You."

How do I feel? (colour in or draw your own)

CONFIDENT   HUNGRY   CLEVER   SERIOUS   EXCITED

Fill in the blank space with your name:

Kiki thinks _____ is clever for doing this journal. Keep going rockstar!

(date)

_____

Today's "Mighty Me" Mission

Balance on your left leg - with your eyes closed!

(Try to do this before breakfast.
Write down how long you did this for in the box)

If you beat your score from last month, colour in the star

"You're stronger than you think."

How do I feel? (colour in or draw your own)

CLEVER   CROSS   HUNGRY   EXCITED   WORRIED

Something good that happened today:

(date)

_____

Today's "Mighty Me" Mission

Dance all out for 2 minutes

(Try to do this before breakfast.
Tick the box if you did this)

"Quitters quit. Winners win."

How do I feel? (colour in or draw your own)

CONFIDENT   SERIOUS   CLEVER   SAD   EXCITED

My favourite season is:

Spring / Summer / Autumn / Winter

(date)

_____

Banjo's Bonus!

Banjo's Fresh Orange Juice

1 orange contains all the vitamin C you need for a day

♥ **4 fresh oranges**

♥ Cut them in half. If you don't have a juicer, stick a fork in the middle of the orange half you cut (the fleshy part) and squeeze it over your glass.

Draw your oranges:

Colour in the star if you made and drank Banjo's Fresh Orange Juice

Kiki's Caring Kids Challenge

ACTS OF KINDNESS

Choose 7 acts of kindness for others from the table opposite. Over the next week you will do 1 every day. Write/draw the one you have chosen in your journal and if you have time, how you felt at the end of the day. Did you learn something? Did you feel different? Did you forget to do it? Will you try it again? You will need to prove you have done them so your grown-up helper can sign them off with a stamp or sticker. (You can always do more if you like.)

Try as hard as you can, and you will earn your Certificate of Achievement at the end of the week* – plus you may notice how much happier and better you feel!!

*Cut out the certificate at the end of this week's section or visit www.kikiandfriends.co.uk to download a free A4 copy (under FREE STUFF) to print out.

ACTS OF KINDNESS

ACT OF KINDNESS	STAMP / STICKER	ACT OF KINDNESS	STAMP / STICKER
Be respectful to your parents		Say "I love you" to someone you love	
Write a thank-you note		Help someone learn a new skill (read, skip, etc.)	
Help wash the car or windows		Make something for a friend or relative	
Be polite (e.g. say thank you)			
Make someone laugh (a joke)		Tidy your room without being asked	
No complaining for a whole day			
Help out in the kitchen		Give someone you care about a hug	
Put away your clothes		Surprise someone with a gift you made	
Make a drink for a grown-up			
Help in the garden		Set the table without being asked	

(date)

_____

My act of kindness today is:
(write or draw it)

Being kind means:

"Caring about others.

Listening to them.

Supporting them with words or actions, like a HUG."

How do I feel? (colour in or draw your own)

CONFIDENT   HUNGRY   CLEVER   SERIOUS   EXCITED

(date)

_____

My act of kindness today is:
(write or draw it)

Being kind means:

*"Not being selfish.
Thinking of the needs of others."*

How do I feel? (colour in or draw your own)

HAPPY   SAD   CREATIVE   WORRIED   CONFIDENT

(date)

_____

My act of kindness today is:

(write or draw it)

Being kind means:

"Thinking about others and not just yourself. Respecting others who care for you."

How do I feel? (colour in or draw your own)

CLEVER   CROSS   HUNGRY   EXCITED   WORRIED

(date)

_____

My act of kindness today is:
(write or draw it)

Being kind means:
"Trying to help others if you can. Maybe by making them happy with a note or surprise."

How do I feel? (colour in or draw your own)

 HAPPY

SAD

 CREATIVE

 WORRIED

 HUNGRY

(date)

_____

My act of kindness today is:
(write or draw it)

Being kind means:

"Not hurting others by bullying or teasing them."

How do I feel? (colour in or draw your own)

CONFIDENT   CROSS   CLEVER   HUNGRY   EXCITED

(date)

_____

My act of kindness today is:

(write or draw it)

Being kind means:

"Including others in your games. Sharing your joy and happiness."

How do I feel? (colour in or draw your own)

HAPPY　　SERIOUS　　CREATIVE　　SAD　　HUNGRY

(date)

_____

My act of kindness today is:
(write or draw it)

Being kind means:

"Bringing joy and sunshine into the lives of others."

How do I feel? (colour in or draw your own)

CONFIDENT   SERIOUS   CLEVER   SAD   EXCITED

Wow! You did 7 nice things for other people. Helping others makes you happier! Cut out your certificate or download it from www.kikiandfriends.co.uk FREE STUFF

A KIND START

INVITATION TO BE KIND TO OTHERS

Congratulations! You have demonstrated that you have the positive and caring attitude you need to help be considerate of others

Certificate of Achievement

This is to certify that

....

has undertaken a 7-day challenge in the Kiki Kindness program and is hereby awarded the invitation to be a caring, unselfish person

Parent/Carer

....

Signed

....

Date ....

Your name

....

Signed

....

Date ....

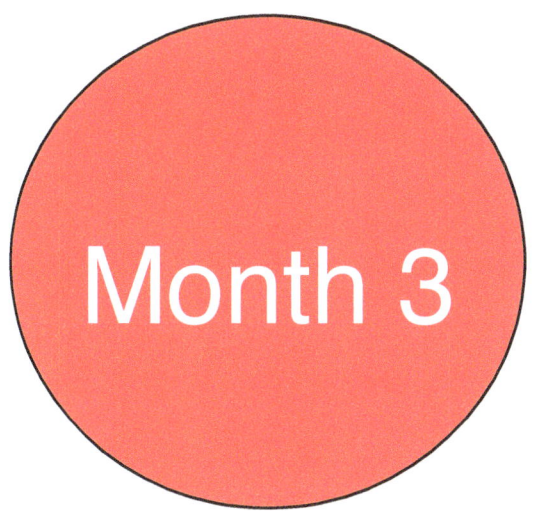

(date)

_____

Kiki's Challenge Week

Today I'm going to

(pick a Kiki Challenge, write it down and read out loud)

_____

What am I looking forward to today?

_____

_____

How do I feel? (colour in or draw your own)

CONFIDENT   HUNGRY   CLEVER   SERIOUS   EXCITED

In the evening: think about your challenge

What did I do differently / learn / find today?

(date)

_____

Kiki's Challenge Week

Today I'm going to

(pick a Kiki Challenge, write it down and read out loud)

_____

What am I looking forward to today?

_____

_____

How do I feel? (colour in or draw your own)

HAPPY   SAD   CREATIVE   WORRIED   CONFIDENT

What did I do differently / learn / find today?

(date)

_____

Kiki's Challenge Week

Today I'm going to

(pick a Kiki Challenge, write it down and read out loud)

_____

What am I looking forward to today?

_____

_____

How do I feel? (colour in or draw your own)

CLEVER   CROSS   HUNGRY   EXCITED   WORRIED

What did I do differently / learn / find today?

(date)

_____

Kiki's Challenge Week

Today I'm going to

(pick a Kiki Challenge, write it down and read out loud)

_____

What am I looking forward to today?

_____

_____

How do I feel? (colour in or draw your own)

HAPPY   SAD   CREATIVE   WORRIED   HUNGRY

What did I do differently / learn / find today?

(date)

_____

Kiki's Challenge Week

Today I'm going to

(pick a Kiki Challenge, write it down and read out loud)

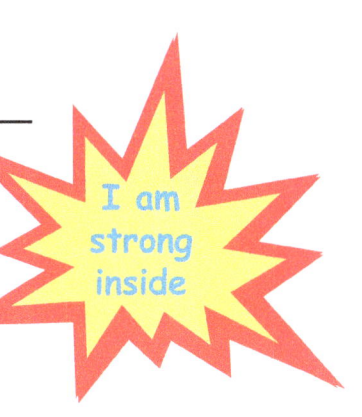

I am strong inside

_____

What am I looking forward to today?

_____

_____

How do I feel? (colour in or draw your own)

CONFIDENT   CROSS   CLEVER   HUNGRY   EXCITED

What did I do differently / learn / find today?

(date)

_____

Kiki's Challenge Week

Today I'm going to

(pick a Kiki Challenge, write it down and read out loud)

I have BIG dreams

_____

What am I looking forward to today?

_____

_____

How do I feel? (colour in or draw your own)

HAPPY   SERIOUS   CREATIVE   SAD   HUNGRY

What did I do differently / learn / find today?

(date)

_____

Kiki's Challenge Week

Today I'm going to

(pick a Kiki Challenge, write it down and read out loud)

_____

What am I looking forward to today?

_____

_____

How do I feel? (colour in or draw your own)

CONFIDENT   SERIOUS   CLEVER   SAD   EXCITED

What did I do differently / learn / find today?

(date)

_____

Dali's Doodle Day

Today I'm going to draw me being brave

(and/or colour in Kiki standing up to Percy)

I want to learn (how to play an instrument, a game, how to swim, or anything you want)

_____

_____

_____

How do I feel? (colour in or draw your own)

CONFIDENT　　HUNGRY　　CLEVER　　SERIOUS　　EXCITED

I am thankful for

_____

_____

_____

Kiki standing up to Percy

Me being brave:

(date)

_____

Dali's Doodle Day

Today I'm going to draw me having fun with my friends

(and/or colour in Edgar, Allan and Poe on their adventure)

I am really good at

_____

_____

_____

How do I feel? (colour in or draw your own)

I am friends with

_____

_____

_____

Edgar, Allan and Poe on their adventure

Me having fun with my friends:

(date)

_____

Dali's Doodle Day

Today I'm going to draw me waving

(and/or colour in Piero waving)

I am really good at

_____

_____

_____

How do I feel? (colour in or draw your own)

CLEVER   CROSS   HUNGRY   EXCITED   WORRIED

I am thankful for

_____

_____

_____

Piero waving

Me waving:

(date)

_____

Dali's Doodle Day

Today I'm going to draw me learning

(and/or colour in Kiki and Banjo learning)

I am really good at

_____

_____

_____

How do I feel? (colour in or draw your own)

HAPPY   SAD   CREATIVE   WORRIED   HUNGRY

The funniest thing I saw or did today:

_____

_____

_____

Kiki and Banjo learning

Me learning:

(date)

_____

Dali's Doodle Day

Today I'm going to draw me listening

(and/or colour in Kiki and Banjo listening politely)

I am really good at

_____

_____

_____

How do I feel? (colour in or draw your own)

CONFIDENT   CROSS   CLEVER   HUNGRY   EXCITED

I am thankful for

_____

_____

_____

Kiki and Banjo listening politely to Lord Byron

Me listening:

(date)

_____

Dali's Doodle Day

Today I'm going to draw me and my favourite "baddies" character(s)

(and/or colour in The Farmies)

I am really good at

_____

_____

_____

How do I feel? (colour in or draw your own)

HAPPY   SERIOUS   CREATIVE   SAD   HUNGRY

The best thing that happened today:

_____

_____

_____

My favourite bad-guy character(s):
(from a comic, film, book or Kiki and Friends)

(date)

_____

Dali's Doodle Day

Today I'm going to draw me at a party
(and/or colour in Kiki and Friends celebrating)

I am really good at

_____

_____

_____

How do I feel? (colour in or draw your own)

CONFIDENT   SERIOUS   CLEVER   SAD   EXCITED

I am thankful for

_____

_____

_____

Kiki and Friends celebrating

Me at a party:

(date)

_____

Today's "Mighty Me" Mission

Jumping Jacks for 1 minute

(Try to do this before breakfast. It's month 3, you're still doing this. You're amazing! Write down how many you did in the box)

If you beat your score from last month, colour in the star

Amazing things happen when you try

How do I feel? (colour in or draw your own)

CONFIDENT   HUNGRY   CLEVER   SERIOUS   EXCITED

Fill in the blank space with your name:

Kiki thinks _____ is amazing at these mighty Missions. Keep going!

(date)

_____

Today's "Mighty Me" Mission

Arm circles for 1 minute

(Both arms at the same time - don't give up, I know it's hard.
Write down how many you did in the box)

If you beat your score from last month, colour in the star

Mistakes are proof you're trying

How do I feel? (colour in or draw your own)

HAPPY   SAD   CREATIVE   WORRIED   CONFIDENT

Something good that happened yesterday:

(date)

_____

Today's "Mighty Me" Mission

Balance on your right leg

(Try to do this before breakfast. You're a mighty me!
Write down how long you did this for in the box)

If you beat your score from last month, colour in the star

Nothing is impossible when you put your mind to it

How do I feel? (colour in or draw your own)

CLEVER   CROSS   HUNGRY   EXCITED   WORRIED

What would you like to be good at when you are 10 years old?

(date)

_____

Today's "Mighty Me" Mission

Balance on your left leg

(Try to do this before breakfast. You're getting good at this!
Write down how long you did this for in the box)

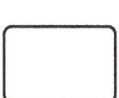

If you beat your score from last month, colour in the star

If at first you don't succeed, try and try again

How do I feel? (colour in or draw your own)

HAPPY   SAD   CREATIVE   WORRIED   HUNGRY

Someone who helped you today:

(date)

_____

Today's "Mighty Me" Mission

Balance on your right leg - with your eyes closed!

(Try to do this before breakfast.
Write down how long you did this for in the box)

If you beat your score from last month, colour in the star

You don't have to be perfect to be amazing

How do I feel? (colour in or draw your own)

CONFIDENT   CROSS   CLEVER   HUNGRY   EXCITED

The funniest thing you saw today:

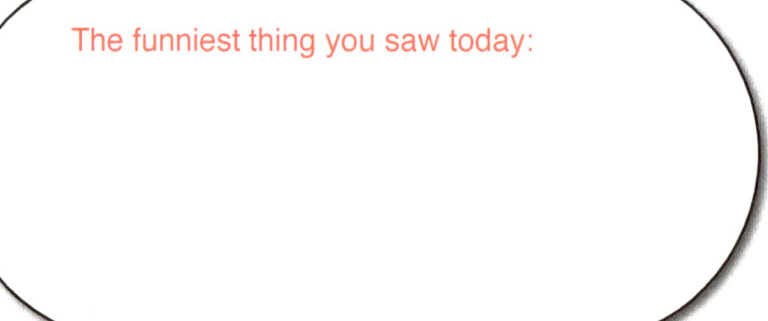

(date)

_____

Today's "Mighty Me" Mission

Balance on your left leg - with your eyes closed!

(Try to do this before breakfast.
Write down how long you did this for in the box)

If you beat your score from last month, colour in the star

Nothing amazing came from a comfort zone

How do I feel? (colour in or draw your own)

A good thing that happened today:

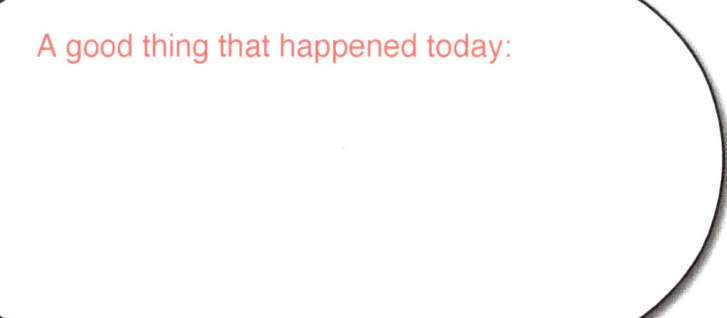

(date)

_____

Today's "Mighty Me" Mission

Dance all out for 2 minutes

(Try to do this before breakfast.
Tick the box if you did this)

**Dancing makes you happy.
Dance your way to happiness.**

How do I feel? (colour in or draw your own)

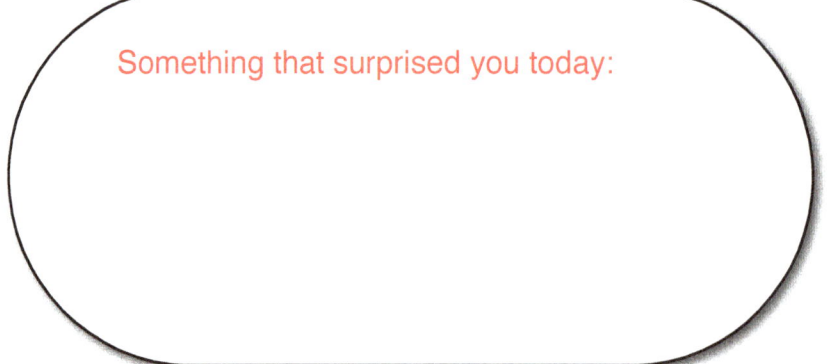

CONFIDENT   SERIOUS   CLEVER   SAD   EXCITED

Something that surprised you today:

You're a Mighty Me champion! You've completed 3 months.
Well done!! Look in the mirror and say: "I am mighty!"

WORDSEARCH WITH KIKI

Look for the 10 words below related to confidence. Words can go left, right, up, down and diagonally - even backwards!

S	H	O	R	A	W	A	R	E	T
C	S	T	R	O	N	G	J	T	O
A	G	H	O	R	E	H	N	V	E
P	F	E	A	R	L	E	S	S	S
A	I	F	N	E	D	N	T	E	M
B	O	L	D	I	M	V	I	V	A
L	M	U	F	R	W	S	E	A	R
E	A	N	L	I	I	U	Q	R	T
X	O	Y	N	P	N	R	Z	B	B
C	R	D	E	T	S	E	N	O	H

BOLD   STRONG
CONFIDENT   CAPABLE
BRAVE   SMART
SURE   HONEST
AWARE   FEARLESS

There are 3 examples highlighted in yellow
WIN (down), WIN, (diagonally) and HERO (backwards).

YOU'RE AMAZING!

Kiki's Caring Kids Challenge

ACTS OF GIVING BACK

Choose 7 acts of giving back to our planet from the table opposite. Over the next week you will do 1 every day. Some take longer, but you still get a sticker or stamp when they are done. Try to choose evenly between those in the left and those in the right column. You will need to prove you have done them so your grown-up helper can sign them off with a stamp or sticker. (You can always do more if you like.)

Try as hard as you can, and you will earn your Certificate of Achievement at the end of the week* – then you will notice how the world around you sparkles more and you get a good feeling inside!!

*Cut out the certificate at the end of this week's section or visit www.kikiandfriends.co.uk to download a free A4 copy (under FREE STUFF) to print out.

ACTS OF GIVING BACK

ACT OF GIVING BACK	STAMP / STICKER
Help recycle waste at home for this whole week	
No new plastic toys for a month	
Recycle your paper + card for this whole week	
Turn the light off when you leave a room, all week	
List 3 ways to be eco-friendly	
Plant your own herbs, salad	
Set up a rain-water collector	
Take shorter showers for this whole week	
List 3 renewable energy types	
Spend time in nature (for 3 days this week)	

ACT OF GIVING BACK	STAMP / STICKER
Learn about an animal - where it lives, what it eats	
Learn about an insect - where it lives, what it eats	
Learn about a tree - where it grows, draw it	
Learn about a flower - where it grows, draw it	
Learn about a fish - where it lives, what it eats	
Learn about coral - where it grows, draw it	
Learn about a whale - where it lives, what it eats	

(date)

_____

Which act of "giving back" to your planet did you do today? (write or draw)

I am caring for the environment and giving back because:

"The world is a beautiful place filled with amazing plants and animals."

How do I feel? (colour in or draw your own)

CONFIDENT   HUNGRY   CLEVER   SERIOUS   EXCITED

(date)

_____

Which act of "giving back" to your planet did you do today? (write or draw)

I am caring for the environment and giving back because:

"I am part of something big. There are children like me all over the world. We are in this together."

How do I feel? (colour in or draw your own)

HAPPY   SAD   CREATIVE   WORRIED   CONFIDENT

(date)

_____

Which act of "giving back" to your planet did you do today? (write or draw)

I am caring for the environment and giving back because:

"If I don't look after the plants, oceans and animals, who will?"

How do I feel? (colour in or draw your own)

CLEVER   CROSS   HUNGRY   EXCITED   WORRIED

_____ (date)

Which act of "giving back" to your planet did you do today? (write or draw)

I am caring for the environment and giving back because:

"The world gives me tasty food, sunshine, beaches and rainbows. It asks for nothing in return."

How do I feel? (colour in or draw your own)

HAPPY   SAD   CREATIVE   WORRIED   HUNGRY

(date)

_____

Which act of "giving back" to your planet did you do today? (write or draw)

I am caring for the environment and giving back because:

"If the world is polluted we won't have any more tasty food, our seas will be too dirty to swim in and the animals will have nowhere to live."

How do I feel? (colour in or draw your own)

CONFIDENT   CROSS   CLEVER   HUNGRY   EXCITED

(date)

_____

Which act of "giving back" to your planet did you do today? (write or draw)

I am caring for the environment and giving back because:

"Animals cannot speak, but they should still be heard.
I am their voice."

How do I feel? (colour in or draw your own)

HAPPY   SERIOUS   CREATIVE   SAD   HUNGRY

(date)

_____

Which act of "giving back" to your planet did you do today? (write or draw)

I am caring for the environment and giving back because:

"I love plants, animals and splashing in water."

How do I feel? (colour in or draw your own)

CONFIDENT   SERIOUS   CLEVER   SAD   EXCITED

Well done! You've spent a whole week learning about and helping the amazing world you live in. Cut out your certificate or print out an A4 poster from www.kikiandfriends.co.uk FREE STUFF

 # THE RIGHT START

INVITATION TO HELP SAVE THE WORLD

Congratulations! You have demonstrated that you have the positive and helpful attitude you need to help look after our planet

Certificate of Achievement

This is to certify that

....

has undertaken a 7-day challenge in the Kiki Give Back program and is hereby awarded the invitation to be one of the world's heroes

Parent/Carer

....

Signed

....

Date

Your name

....

Signed

....

Date ....

BONUS SECTION

You can now list the
top 3 things*

I am thankful for:

_____

_____

_____

I am good at:

_____

_____

_____

I look forward to:

_____

_____

_____

* You've already listed these. Look back in your journal to choose if you like

What colour makes you feel happiest?

(you can colour the balloon in your favourite colour!)

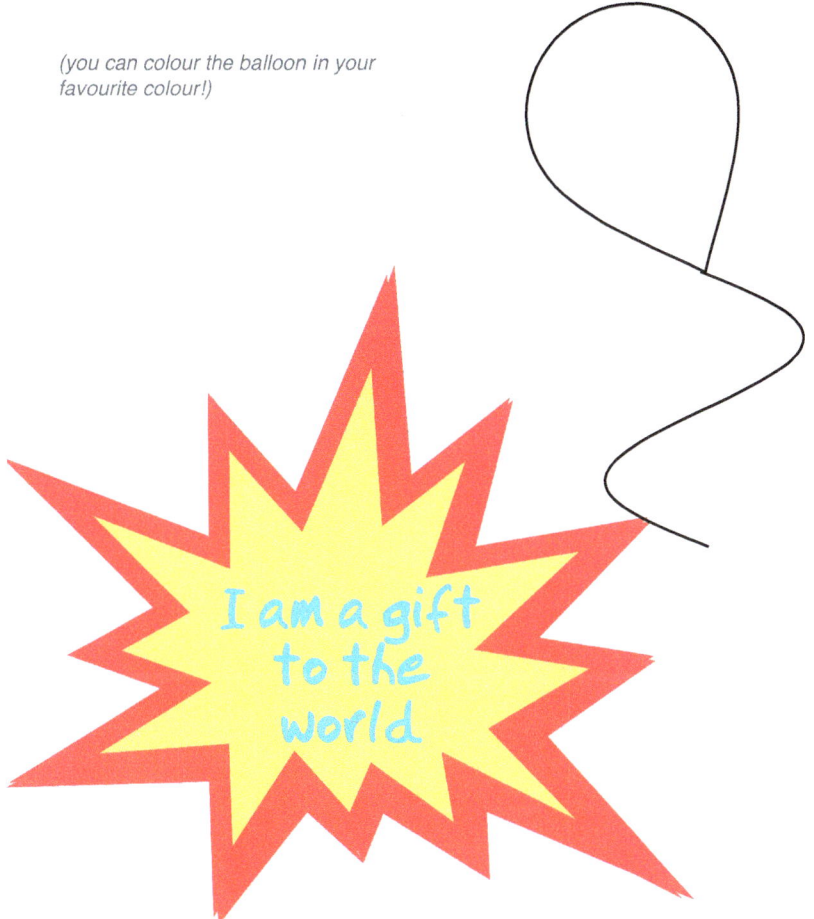

YOU ARE AMAZING!

.... find out why on the next page

The things that make you SPECIAL

FAMILY HISTORY
- Where your family is from
- Where you were born
- Where you were raised
- Who raised you
- Important people in your life
- Who you were closest to

My Culture
- Traditions
- Race
- Beliefs
- Language(s)

MEMORIES
- Places you visited
- Favourite memories
- Games and activities
- Who you spent time with
- Things you collected

My Hobbies
Activities you enjoy and that give you a sense of purpose

My Characteristic Traits
I AM...
Your positive qualities that make you proud of who you are and what others enjoy about you.

Ways I Feel Better
- People, places, things and activities that bring joy and comfort
- Coping skills
- Relaxation
- Fun stuff

My Biology
- Physical appearance (e.g. curly hair, short legs, round face, tall)
- Illness
- Gender
- Physical abilities

My Choices
- My positive thoughts
- Why I love life
- Why I believe in me

My Dreams & Wishes
- What you want for your future
- Hopes for your education and career
- Experiences you dream about having in the future

My Talents
Skills you developed over time or are learning with practice.

Use the above to help you colour in and fill out YOU
or draw out your own A4 version

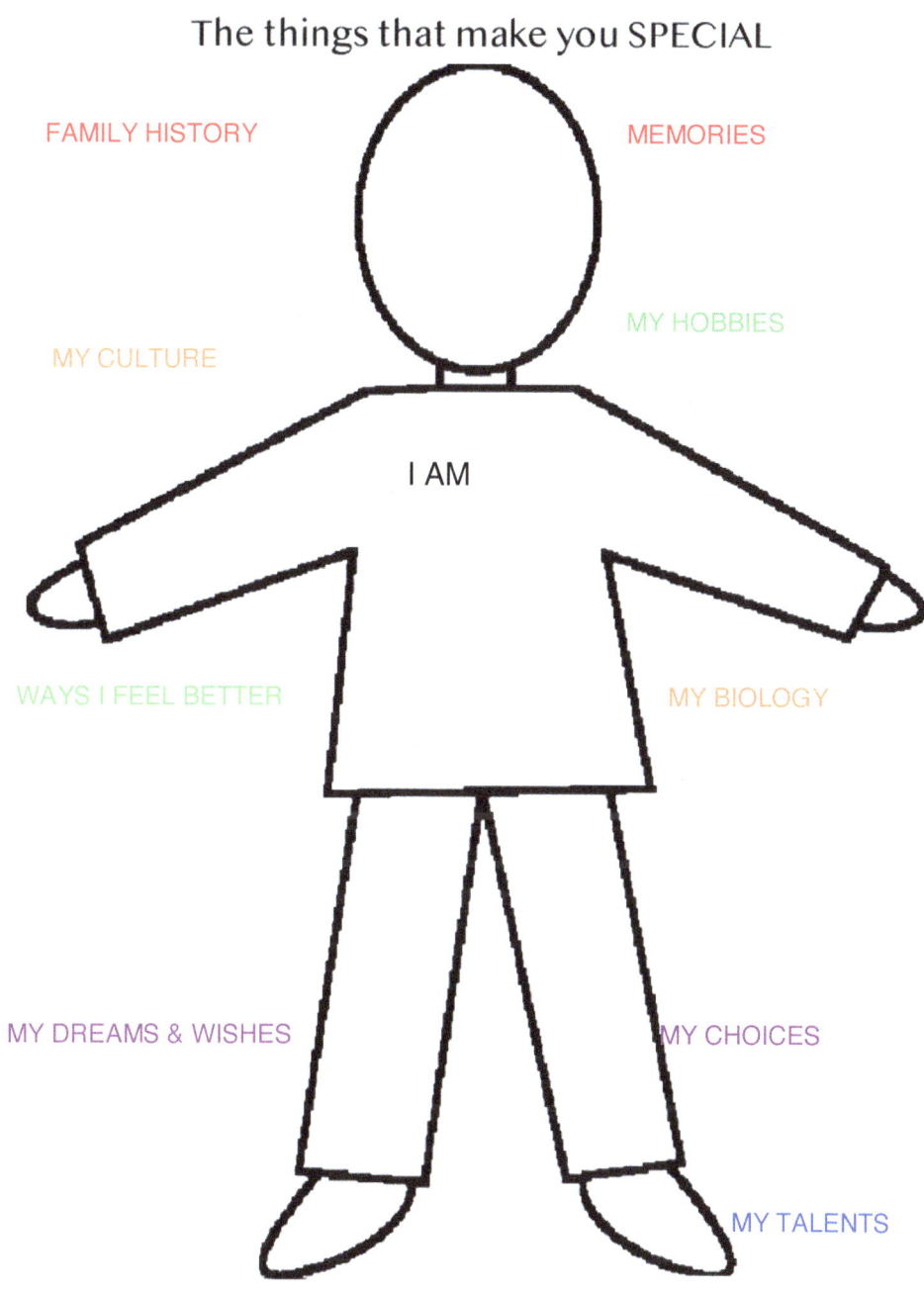

Believing in myself is my superpower

Published by: Babili Books, UK
Copyright ©2020 Francesca Hepton

www.ingramcontent.com/pod-product-compliance
Lightning Source LLC
Chambersburg PA
CBHW040416100526
44588CB00022B/2841